# *Deepest & Darkest*

## Ginger Lee

# opyright

Copyright © 2023 by Ginger Lee
Copyright © 2021 by Ginger Lee
Copyright © 2020 by Ginger Lee

All rights reserved. No part of this publication may be reproduced, distributed, or transmitted in any form or by any means, without prior written permission.

Author website: gleewrites.com

This is a work of fiction. Any resemblance to actual people, living or dead is completely coincidental.

Cover by RJ Creatives
Formatting by My Notes in the Margin

✿ Created with Vellum

She welcomes
The nightmare he is
Her lover brings
The deepest darkest
Parts of him
And she wraps them up
Tied with black string

Straddling hips
Her neck is introduced to his lips
His fist winds round her hair
She's almost there
She's unsure if she has heaven or hell between her knees
But what he gives
Makes her eager to please

Break a few ribs
I can't take it anymore
The flapping and flapping
These wings of my heavy heart
Struggling to be free
Letting it go will be the hardest part

She wears his words
Draped across her collarbone
With wanton whispers
Trailed by kisses
From worshiping lips

Warm lips with a destination
Vibrating over moans
Making promises only to her

Pass me the lighter
This candle won't burn itself

Every meaningful encounter
Should end with a wistful sigh

Lips gravitate towards the nearest neck

Some secrets stay comfortably within my soul
Memories made with lovers muddle my mind
The feeling of your fingertips still fluttering across my skin
Hot breath in my ear and love lingering behind your eyes

She puts it on
Just so
He
Can
Slowly
Take it off

From her, he constantly fed
Hunger and cravings never ceasing
He drank from each place she offered
No other would satisfy the need
Unified by the universe
No one could ever break the bond
Together forever
At the edge of the world

My burning heart bleeds into a cup
I drain myself all for him
And feel ecstasy till the very end

My tongue is a weapon
And your heart, it bleeds

Take me in small doses
A little at a time
If you don't overdo it
I'll make you feel oh so fine

Don't extinguish this flame
Make me burn brighter

Creatures of the night only
Come with me
Let's play truth or scare

Your fangs, my neck

Hot girl summer is over
It's time for
Cardigan wearing
Coffee drinking
Weird girl Fall

Me and the moon
And bat wings
And brooms

Wait till the wind blows
Wait till the rain comes
Keep watch
My time is coming
You may be ready
But I am not
The clouds will make me whole
Resurrect me in the midst of the storm

So many memories playing on repeat
I'm obsessed with the bad times as much as I am the good
I cut out your eyes from the selfie we took
Your beautiful eyes in my favorite shade of blue
Stuck to my wall with the knife you used

The pretty dolls on the dusty shelf
See through the lies you tell yourself
Don't let others enter
The dolls will confess
The evil deeds done
The things you hid in the chest
Burn it
Burn it
Burn the house down
Silence their whispers
And get out of town

Your reputation precedes you, sir
Your devilish deeds are just what we're looking for
Terribly twisted acts of an infamous magician
Will leave your prey shocked, breathless and in complete submission

Stifled cries
I bit my lip
The taste of blood
I whispered
"Don't quit"
He held down my hips
And I squirmed
Surrendering to his serpentine tongue

I'm not a moth drawn to your scorching flame
I'm the lit match to your wanting wick

Play me like a piano
Fingers that bring
Sweet music out of me
I will follow your pace
I will sing like a dream

You don't know what your darkness does to me my love

Pull me down on the cool sheets
Skim your fingers from neck to feet
Give me goosebumps
Light my flame
Call me baby
I'm yours to tame

Lovers touching fingers to lips
The world on fire witnessing the sins they commit

Give me the world
The world in your head
The world in your heart
Make me your world

The look warranted a lick
The neck enjoyed a trick
The tongue played a melody of perfect pitch

He smelled like longing and want and pure lust

Sliding, gliding
Moonlight glows
Hiding, finding
Emotions grow
Whispers, moaning
Skin touching skin
Surrendering willingly
Take me again

Her bottom lip was his sweet salvation

Hot palms find curves then slide to the place above my hips
Fingers grip and pull me closer
His hands are occupied while mine appreciate his jawline
So that I can tease his lips

He was thirsty for her pretty poison

Wanting her wasn't an option
Loving her came easy
Keeping her was his goal
He no longer felt lost
She possessed his soul

It's more than a need
It's a craving

It hurt in just the right way
Begged for more
Pleaded for pain
Pleasure for sure

A mischievous wink then
Warm lips press against mine
Beneath your heavy weight
My body burns
The seductive feel
Of fingers intertwining
I come undone

I desire to be put in such a state
Where my need is met
My want is extinguished
My boundaries are shattered
My body spent

Roll over
My body
Like billowing clouds
Caress my slick skin
Like thrumming
Laps of erotic current
Drag me
Under the weight of you

A rush of blood
I blushed
Your mouth
Was crushed
With lips
That hushed
Being wicked
With trust

My fingers are itching to be on you
I want to dip my hands in your pools of desire
To unravel your darkest fantasy
To watch your face when you close your eyes
Completely satisfied

Come hither, my dear

I offer a moan and a curse
As he breaks me in the best way

The finger he trailed down her spine
Led them both to heaven

The twisted game she plays ends up with you around her finger

His taste on my tongue
Hands in my hair
I hum as his groan floats through the air

Save him for last
He loves the wait
I like to savor my favorite
He leaves a lovely taste

Adore him like a saint
Ravage him like the sinner he is

Her nectar, so sweet
He couldn't help but partake

Welcoming eyes
Consume me sighs

I'd be a fool not to accept the offer
Of a sip of you

No, no, darling
She's not devoted
Her need is carnal
Teetering towards obsession

Clenching and gnashing
Caught between teeth

A wicked whisper
A dark devotion
A pretty possession
Completes my collection

Be a sinner or a saint
We could all use
A little more
Darkness or light

You must offer your soul
According to the rules of the game

I clawed the sand
The breath left my lungs
As you dragged me down
I felt your fingers
They learned every inch of me
I tasted the salt on your lips
Your body was heavy and warm
The sea cold and lonely
It repossessed you
I watched you slip under the waves

She told him once
"I'm not heaven sent. I clawed my way out of hell for you"

He missed her body
That flower that bloomed in the dark
Just for him

If you pull me into a dark corner
Be ready for a fight
If a kiss I don't receive
Before you push me back into the light

Lead me into the dark
The hours between midnight and dawn
Fingers entwine like vines
Feet treading atop moss
We find the hollowed-out tree
Our spot
Curling up, body molding to body
The fire between us
Melting into one

My darkness meets your darkness in the twisted place where my daydreams touch your nightmares

Thoughts penetrate the dark
All my hope fades
Despair seeps in
Emptying my heart
A light pierced through
I searched the black void
To focus on the silhouette of you
Hope trickles back in
The muscle beats again

When it's late at night
And your mind is running wild
Chasing dreams but awake
Alone with your emotions
Heart about to break

Pick the most beautiful shadow and fade away far into the darkness

Fast fading prick of thorns
The sting of regret remains
Thoughts of you wrapped around my heart
Is the most wanted pain

He watched her walk away
And felt the pain of his words on his lips

The well of my soul has run dry
There is no more you and I
Your feelings are cold
This pain has grown old
Our story of true love
Will never be told

When will you let go?
This hold on my heart
Or maybe it's me holding on
Too weak to forget
Afraid I'll fall apart

Be careful with me
When your hand grasps mine to pull me up
The rest of me will fall to pieces

My shaken soul is growing weary
You stomp me down
Then hold me dearly
You play the game
And then release me
I need a lover who would die to keep me

A head thick with thoughts

We are like a fish and a bird
Never to be

Stripped of all my feelings
All of me laid bare
My heart and soul
Have been exposed
I have nothing
Left to share

Lips sealed
Tongue tied
Soul crushed
Mind numbed
But my heart is boiling over

Broken but better for it

Love me to the moon and leave me there

Bare feet on moss
Pine and sweet grass linger in the atmosphere
His hand grabs my wrist
Twirling me around as I turn to cling to him
He holds me
Strong and sensual
He caught me and I am his

Blushing is a telltale sign

If I met you a thousand years ago
My heart would write you a song
If you reached for my hand in the darkness
My soul to you would belong
If you entered my dreams on the coldest nights
My body to you would be sworn
If you loved me at my loneliest
My spirit would be reborn

The deepest part of me
Holds a little piece of you

I'm crawling under the Persian rug with the dust and spider bones for self-care

I threw myself against the brick hearth
In hopes you would sweep up my pieces

I'll sweep myself under the rug again along with the dust, so you won't have to look at me and remember the nights when we were together

Sweep me under your rug
Pull me out when you are lonely

Oh, we've done that
In my dreams

Some things are impossible
And that's okay

You are like the black clouds in my night
Don't be mistaken
I love the dark the best

Don't mind me after midnight

She's a handful wrapped in lust

Her hips sway in that pretty little way
His mouth curves up as she walks away

You're trouble
And I'm the plot twist

An unwritten love story
Told with lush lips
Watching her walk
A sway of hips
A glance over the shoulder
The tale begins
A darkened corner awaits
A moment of escape
Warm palms touching curves
Appeasement deserved

His smile held lust and I was a lucky girl

Romanticizing the simplest glance

Sins confessed
Every time he said her name

She shifted ever-so-slightly and he smelled her vanilla ponytail as it brushed his arm
He resisted planting his hungry mouth on her bare skin
It was so close
That glowing silken shoulder

That sweet way he absently touches her in a room full of people
The heated hand on her back, her arm, her knee
He doesn't even know he's doing it

If your hands hold her just right
You'll never have to ask her for a damn thing

Sinning together is more fun

That dress slid to the floor and his hands ached to explore

Love beyond boundaries
The stars know our names

It was a slip
I think I tripped
I apologize sir
To find ourselves nose to nose
Do you feel these feelings stir?


Our eyes are locked
I breathe your scent
Your lips curve up
Your eyes, they squint


We laugh together
We know where this is moving toward
I'm so glad I fell forward

I love all of you
And I will love you
Beyond the confines
Of this world
I will never stop
My affections will be
Forever present
Hold on to me
And I will never let go

I'm made up of a little bit romantic notion and a whole lot of sighing

Some say you're obsessed
But that's not it
You've found the key
A vital, basic necessity for fulfillment
You're actually grabbing onto something or someone
Holding on for dear life because it matters so much
It fills your holes
You are enough on your own
But this key elevates you

It really matters in life
What you know
Who you know
And knowing when to say no

I believe you can save a person
Just by listening when they need to be heard

Hold this string
It's attached to my dream

I'm in the mood for a threesome with the ghost that wakes me up at 3am and the thoughts inside my head

A lust for books

So magical, she falls to pieces with beauty and grace

The man in the tree
He stares at me
He keeps watch whenever I leave
I only see his glowing eyes
Always in a darkened sky
I fear his face will soon be shown
As fall removes the foliage grown
The howling wind warns to go back in
Stay inside till winter's end

My cup of coffee knows all my secrets

Making out in the mezzanine

Do tentacles seem to slither or more like wiggle?
I want to get this memoir just right

Music and curvy roads help me keep my head on straight

Music is the water
I am the stone
It slowly wears away
And I welcome it

What if negative words tasted terrible and positive words tasted heavenly?
How beautifully we would speak

My good eye is my third eye

I want to crawl on my hands and knees over a thick moss forest floor
Pausing to press a cheek on the cool dampness
Inhaling earth and dew

"What a creature you are"
She whispered in his ear
His eyelids closed tight as he leaned in
Nuzzling her exposed neck
Taking in her sweet scent
So he could remember the moment
She seemed to purr at the touch
Knowing his desire ran deep
She knew his mouth
Wherever it ventured
Would make her warm
Passion driven kisses along her collarbone
Her fingers found pleasure
In the soft shortness of his hair
He moaned
Wishing for this to be
His eternal damnation

My eyes will shine as two flames
On the darkest nights
Curves illuminated
By the full moonlight
Your heartbeat will quicken
Feeling sensual fear
Carnal desire captivates

Many a beast
Hide under my feet
The snarls you'll hear
When I draw near

Her last breath was a sigh

The whole world watched
As I withered away
Without your love
I became decay
Back to the earth
My body belonged
A lost spirit floated free
Haunted and wronged

Crunching leaves and a familiar chanting murmur drifts through barren trees
A smell of smoke and burning oak wood is carried by the breeze
My senses perk up as I spy my other half in supplication to the moon
Closer still I long to tend to hidden wounds
My need grows and desire builds filling every part of me
Reunited at last I cling to him as I fall onto my knees

I clenched my jaw
And heard a crow caw
The spices prepared
Filled putrid air
My beloved's silent body
Lay very still
Soon to be buried
On the highest hill
The place we were to become
One flesh and bone
Tragically now
I was alone

I found it first
Leftover from the hunt
Discarded but meat still
Left on the bone
My mate soon arrived
He followed my scent, clever fellow
I already partook, but left him the marrow

My bed doesn't feel like my bed
Something is off in my head
The body it lays
Weighed down
No fingertips tapping
Not one toe twitch
A scream will not be heard
Paralysis of the tongue
If I catch a breath
I'll know I'm alive
This night, I may not survive

Tick tick
Tick tick
Gears turn
Click click
Burning and yearning
The metal man's heart
Loved his creator
From the very start

Such a sweet bird
A rare beauty indeed
Fitting to be admired
By the king
A quiet demeanor
Under a guise
Her offerings are twisted
Fulfilling desires
Her cage, his bedchamber
But pity, she does not need
His darkness delights her
No wish to be free

An envelope closed with a wax seal
Never opened by her delicate fingers
Gathering dust from days
Then weeks
Then months where it lays
The contents forgotten
Something she will not see
Words written on paper
Now the broken pieces of me

To love so deeply
To feel so much
Then they leave
The pain
It cuts
Their name is left
On the tip of your tongue
Unholy thirst
An endless curse

The girl loved the wolf
The wolf loved her blood
His human form
Brought lustful delight
But he took her life
When day turned to night

Forlorn words
Spoken with soft lips
Uttered on the wind
Float over my final resting place
This past body of mine
Under the earth
While you stand here
Alive and taking a breath
I will find you
In the next life
My darling

A haunting list
Rolled up in my clenched fist
Pull the covers up high
For you, I'm coming to spy
I promise to be nice
Just don't look at me twice

Goosebumps come
His breath
It escalates
Watching her from the woods
Shadows obnubilate
He wants it badly
But always waits
Sweet flesh too innocent
To take a taste

The lantern light glowed
Sand between my toes
Fingers intertwined
He said he would be mine
I gave him everything
Every heartbeat
Every kiss
How was I to know
This would be the last night
I was his

I smoothed my palm
Across the crisp linen cloth
Then placed it in my lap
A woman in midnight blue
Delivered a goblet
Of smokey caliginous juice
Cool crystal kissed my lips
As I sipped then drank it down
I had ordered the most potent poison
Very soon I wouldn't be around

Forever dwelling
Behind iron gates
Side by side gravestones
They made perfect mates
The spirit of the boy
The spirit of the girl
Till the end of everything
To haunt and toil

Tales only, they may be
Of bats and vampires
And creaking old houses
And I, carrying a candlestick lit
Padding up rickety steps
To meet the dark one
Waiting at the top for me

Wicked whispers all around
As he led her through the crowd
A scandalous affair indeed
Her fragile mortality intrigued
As respected primus of the brood
He made sure she did not become the food

The witches have your name
Sliding through their lips
The rum has them dancing
And swaying iniquitous hips
The chanting grows louder
And your fate, it tips

Much like a dream
He never wanted to wake from
The evanescence of her silhouette
Lingered in his bedroom
He still smelled her perfume
On the pillowcase
But she was not here
Like a ghost
He wished would make itself known
By rattling the chandelier

A long dark corridor
Is meant to be explored
With creaking floors
And thick wooden doors
Clicking of locks
With a turn of the skeleton key
What lies behind them
Remains to be seen

The owl's favorite spot
Perched upon a skull
Gathering up squeaking mice
Soon his belly is full
All through the night
From cranium to field he flies
Talons snatching up tiny creatures
Until the moonlight dies

The stories told by the aged harridan
Frightened feral children of the town
Ghosts and goblins and ghastly things
Described in such grotesque and gruesome detail
Kept them from wandering out of bounds

Wails coming from the attic
But she hasn't been
Locked up there
In so long
Maybe it's the
Horrible memories
Of all the ways
She was wronged

If bedlam is what you seek
Look no further
The wild things come here
To torment and tease
With scalpels and blood on their sleeves
Nightmares and dreams
For some, peace
For others, screams

Numb and at rest
Eyes blink then a breath
Slow heart beating
Within this cavernous chest
"Give me the leeches"
Just one simple request
I wish to feel something
Anything, please
Sometimes pain is best

It's not for the faint of heart
Please look away for the next part
My scalpel makes the cut
With a steady hand slicing through
I cauterize the oozing
Minimizing loss is what I do
Expert removal of disease
Finally stitching you up, perfectly neat

I will offer an apprentice higher pay
For I do not keep hours during the day
They must not be easily queasy
The…job I perform
Well, it isn't easy
You see, it's in the shadows
Where dangerous demons lurk
And special skills are required for this work

The word creature
Suggests he was created
That's precisely what I've done
A perfect laboratory specimen
Starting my lover's life over
It has begun
He will cherish and remember me
From the happy times gone by
I excised very particular amygdala
In formaldehyde it now lies

Safety first
Is my motto
When you come
To me for healing
I solemnly swear
The straps are there
For your wellbeing

You picked your poison
Now drink it down
The medicine chosen
Will help you drown
Quietly and peacefully
Slowly falling asleep
Sinking under the waves
Final rest in the deep

Would you give me your attention  
If I was an anomaly  
Beautifully odd and different  
Pulling out desire uncommonly

Sir, I need a tonic
Not one I would normally find
I'm in search of the perfect elixir
To make the gentleman mine

Ether held to the nose
Take a deep breath in
A gruesome gathering
A surgical spectacle to begin
You lay in lethargy
The theatre is packed
The surgeons are ready
Quickly bestowing your femur a whack
Your eyes fly open
As the flutist's fingers flit
You'll never forget the taste
Of the leather strap you bit

Yes, a tourniquet on every extremity
That's right
I'm losing my limbs to this illness
I planned it this way
Having them cut off
Only needing my head and my heart
All of the rest will rot and decay

An extract of this
A sliver of that
Dashes of spice
Pinches of bat
This brew boils
A scent so divine
Easy to swallow
Much like sweet wine
I don't blame you
For taking it all
You couldn't have known
It would bring such trauma
My secret ingredient
Is the purple belladonna

"Mercy!" the nurse cried
As the wild-eyed bewildered doctor
Pulled the kicking screaming
Creature from my womb
Others in the suite gasped
As I, spent and sweating from labor
Sat up and reached for him, my odd boy
And a mother's love bloomed

This requiem I have written
Long before I've gone
Will be read by the man in the moon
Out on the starlit lawn
I wish for my ashes to be spread
Along the edge of the dark pond
Precisely at the stroke of midnight
And the mourners
Shall weep until dawn

Her ears perked up
As sounds of small
Nocturnal creatures
Dotted the forest floor
And high upon limbs
The owls watched
Under moonlight
As her whiskers and nose twitched
Ready to pounce
This Machiavellian feline forager

Black as pitch
Curled up in corners
Stygian shadows
Consume
It is in these places
Where comfort cradles me
And infinite ideas
Bloom

Love like a cellar
Dark and dim and cold
A creeping crawling lust
Dirty and rotten and bold
Desire and need in all forms
Forging an oddly bond
Soulmates bound forever
Into the grave and beyond

With my unbelieving eyes
Your shadow passed
I watched it travel along the walls
I pulled the quilt up over my nose
Trying not to make the slightest noise
It stopped and stared at the foot of my bed
But it can't be you for you are dead

This grave hugs me like a forgotten friend
Oh, the restful slumber I've been longing for is finally here
A chant to call upon the rolling fog
It obliges and comes over me like a blanket
Night sounds lull me to sweet sleep
Unmatched peace is found behind the cemetery gates

I'm finding it hard to breathe
This thick air filled with dust
Settling over everything
Even me
The moon is out
But it is dark here
And the silence
Rings in my ears
There is nothing to see
They moved on
And left desolate walls
Where family photographs hung

# About the Author

Ginger Lee, romance novelist and dark poet, spends her days raising her daughter, traveling with her husband, and attending concerts with friends. She is an avid reader and coffee & vampire enthusiast who collects art, movies, Monster High Dolls and oddities. In her free time, she enjoys walks through the neighborhood and thrift store shopping. Ginger loves to connect with other authors, readers, and the writing community on social media.

*How to Contact Ginger Lee*

- Email: gleewrites@gmail.com
- Website: gleewrites.com
- www.twitter.com/glee_writes
- www.instagram.com/authorgingerlee
- https://ko-fi.com/gingerlee
- https://allauthor.com/author/gleewrites/.
- www.goodreads.com/gleewrites
- www.facebook.com/gingerweather
- Amazon:

www.ingramcontent.com/pod-product-compliance
Lightning Source LLC
LaVergne TN
LVHW051635080426
835511LV00016B/2345